easy sushi rolls
and miso soups

easy sushi rolls
and miso soups

Fiona Smith Photography by Diana Miller

RYLAND
PETERS
& SMALL

LONDON NEW YORK

Published in the United States in 2004
by Ryland Peters & Small, Inc.
519 Broadway, 5th Floor, New York,
NY 10012
www.rylandpeters.com

10 9 8 7 6 5 4 3 2 1

Library of Congress Cataloging-in-
Publication Data

Smith, Fiona.
  Easy sushi rolls and miso soups / Fiona
Smith ; photography by Diana
Miller.
      p. cm.
Includes index.
  ISBN 1-84172-578-1
  1. Cookery (Fish) 2. Sushi. I. Title.
  TX747.S557 2004
  641.6'92--dc22

        2003016012

Senior Designer Steve Painter
Commissioning Editor
          Elsa Petersen-Schepelern
Editor Susan Stuck
Production Deborah Wehner
Art Director Gabriella Le Grazie
Publishing Director Alison Starling

Food Stylist Lucy McKelvie
Prop Stylist Hélène Lesur

Author's acknowledgments
Thank you so very much to my mother
Naomi and my editor Elsa for all their
help and support.
Thanks also to Lucy McKelvie, Helen
Lesur, Diana Miller, and Steve Painter for
making the food look gorgeous.
I am very grateful to Koji Maruura, from
Japan Mart in Auckland, who helped me
so much with advice and ingredients.

Notes
• All spoon measurements are level
unless otherwise specified.
• All eggs are large unless otherwise
specified. Uncooked or partially
cooked eggs should not be served to
the very young, the very old, those with
compromised immune systems, or
to pregnant women.
• Japanese ingredients are now widely
available in larger supermarkets, natural
food stores, and Asian markets.

contents

serving sushi rolls

Sushi has come a long way in a relatively short time. It always amazes me to think how the mystique surrounding this style of food kept it from being a favorite of home cooks for so long.

But how things have changed! Fresh sushi can be found everywhere from restaurants to supermarkets and fast-food outlets. It is served at elegant parties and the simplest home gatherings. Travel-weary tourists choose sushi restaurants for comforting, familiar food. Children have it in their lunchboxes, and even some school cafeterias serve it. Sushi has become this generation's healthy convenience food.

Techniques used in making sushi can be simplified for the home cook. One of the most popular styles, rolled sushi (maki-zushi) is easy and fun to make at home and, as soon as the process of rolling the rice has been mastered, a world of filling options becomes available. These days, our supermarkets are full of all kinds of sushi ingredients.

Sushi-making utensils and ingredients

Special sushi-making utensils and authentic ingredients are beautiful and useful, and sold even in supermarkets. Many brands of nori come pretoasted and in a variety of grades—use the best you can.

Some of the recipes in this book call for only half a sheet. When this is so, cut the sheets in half from the shortest side, so you are left with the most width. When making rolled sushi remember that rice is easier to handle with wet hands and nori is better to handle with dry. Keep a bowl of vinegared water and a towel on hand to make the job easier.

Serving sushi

Traditional accompaniments for sushi are soy sauce, wasabi, and pickled ginger, often served with miso soup. A smear of wasabi can elevate a piece of sushi from the ordinary to something extraordinary. I have indicated when I think wasabi is important in a recipe. If you do not want to add it in the sushi, serve a small pile on the side, or serve the sushi with a small dish of plain soy and one of wasabi and soy mixed together. Bought wasabi varies immensely; it is possible to find paste with a high percentage of real wasabi, but many are mostly horseradish—once again, buy the best you can or make your own (page 62).

Sushi is traditionally served immediately, but if you have to keep it for a while, wrap uncut rolls in plastic wrap. Keep in a cool place, but NOT in the refrigerator, which will make the rice hard and unpleasant—the vinegar in the rice will help preserve it for a short time.

cooking rice

The key to making sushi is the rice—vinegared rice, or *sumeshi*. Authentic Japanese sushi rice is widely available now, so there is no need to compromise. It has a slightly rounder grain and is stickier than regular long-grain rice, so it will hold together better. Never put cooked sushi rice in the refrigerator—it will become hard and unpleasant. Instead, keep it covered in a cool place. The vinegar will help preserve it.

seasoned sushi rice

1¾ cups sushi rice (short grain)*

2-inch strip of kombu (dried kelp)*

vinegared seasoning

3 tablespoons rice vinegar

4 teaspoons sugar

½ teaspoon salt

makes 4 cups

Various kinds of dried seaweed, such as kombu, nori, and wakame, as well as sushi rice and sushi-making equipment, are available in larger supermarkets, health food stores, and Japanese stores.

To make the vinegared seasoning, put the rice vinegar, sugar, and salt in a small bowl and stir until dissolved. (Doing this first gives it time to dissolve.)

Put the rice in a colander and wash under cold running water, shaking the rice around to ensure it is washed well. Let drain for 30 minutes (this starts the grains absorbing water).

Transfer the rice to a medium saucepan, add the kombu, and cover with 1½ cups water. Bring to a boil, stirring, then reduce to a very low simmer. Cover and cook without stirring for 10 minutes. Remove from the heat and set aside, covered, for 10 minutes.

Transfer the rice to a large, non-metal bowl—traditionally a flat wooden tub called a *hangiri*—and remove the kombu. Pour the vinegared seasoning over the rice and, using a wooden rice paddle or wooden spoon, cut the seasoning through the rice, cutting and turning the rice for about 2 minutes. Take care not to mash the grains (you will feel it become stickier as you turn it).

Cover the rice with a damp cloth and let cool to room temperature before using. Do not refrigerate.

Futo-maki (thick rolled) sushi are great for lunch, because they are more substantial than *hosi-maki* (thin rolled). However, they aren't ideal for fingerfood, because they are more than one mouthful.

five-color roll

½ oz. dry gourd*

2 teaspoons salt, for rubbing

1 cup dashi or fish stock

2 teaspoons Japanese soy sauce

2 teaspoons mirin (sweetened Japanese rice wine)

1 teaspoon sugar

3 large eggs

a pinch of salt

2 teaspoons peanut oil

1½ cups spinach leaves, washed

3 sheets of nori

½ recipe seasoned sushi rice (page 9)

1 small red bell pepper, halved, seeded, and cut into fine strips

1 medium carrot, grated or very thinly sliced

a 20-inch skillet with a lid

makes 24

Gourd (kampyo or calabash) is sold dried in Japanese shops. It is a common ingredient in rolled sushi, and worth trying.

Fill a bowl with water, add the gourd, rub the salt into the gourd to wash it, then drain and rinse thoroughly. Cover the gourd with fresh water and soak for 1 hour. Drain, then put in a saucepan, cover with boiling water, and cook for 5 minutes. Drain, return to the pan, then add the dashi, 1 teaspoon of the soy, 1 teaspoon of the mirin, and the sugar. Bring to a boil, reduce the heat, and simmer for 5 minutes. Let cool in the liquid, then drain.

Put the eggs in a bowl, add the salt and remaining soy and mirin, and mix well. Heat the oil in the pan or skillet over medium heat. Pour in the eggs, swirling the pan so the mixture covers the base. Cook for 2–3 minutes, gently gathering in the cooked omelet around the edges to let the uncooked egg run onto the hot pan. When the egg is set, take off the heat and fold in the 4 sides, so they meet in the middle and the omelet is now double thickness and square. Remove to a board, let cool, then slice into 3 strips.

Wipe out and reheat the pan. Add the washed but still wet spinach and cover with a lid. Cook for 1½–2 minutes until wilted. Tip into a colander and let cool for a few minutes. Using your hands, squeeze out the liquid from the spinach.

Put 1 sheet of nori on a rolling mat, rough side up, and spread with one-third of the rice, leaving 1 inch of nori bare at the far edge. Put a strip of omelet in the middle and put one-third of the gourd, spinach, pepper, and carrot, laid in lengthwise strips on top. Carefully roll up the nori in the mat, pressing the ingredients into the roll as you go. Wet the bare edge of nori and finish rolling to seal. Repeat to make 3 rolls, then cut each one into 8 pieces. Serve with your choice of sushi accompaniments.

vegetarian

A thinly sliced ribbon of zucchini makes a stunning alternative to nori on the outside of a sushi roll. It is easiest to cut the zucchini and beet with a mandoline—the plastic Japanese ones are marvelous and inexpensive—but if you don't have one you can use a good sharp peeler or knife and a steady hand.

pickled zucchini roll
with beet sashimi

1 cup rice vinegar

⅓ cup sugar

2 tablespoons mirin (sweetened Japanese rice wine)

3 medium zucchini or yellow squash, or both

1–2 very small beets or 5–6 baby beets, uncooked

1 teaspoon wasabi paste

1½ tablespoons Japanese mayonnaise

½ recipe seasoned sushi rice (page 9)

dipping sauce

2 tablespoons Japanese mild soy sauce

1 tablespoon sake

makes 18

To make the pickling mixture, put the vinegar, sugar, and mirin in a small saucepan and bring to a boil, stirring. Reduce to a simmer and cook for 5 minutes. Remove from the heat and let cool.

Thinly slice the zucchini and/or squash lengthwise, discarding the first and last couple of pieces (they will be too narrow). Arrange the slices flat in a shallow dish or container and pour the pickling mixture over the top. Set aside for 4 hours or overnight.

When ready to assemble the sushi, peel the raw beets and slice them carefully, as thinly as possible.

Put the wasabi and mayonnaise in a small bowl and mix well.

Divide the seasoned rice into 18 portions about the size of a walnut, and shape each piece into a flattened ball. Wrap a ribbon of pickled zucchini around the outside of each piece, then top with a dab of wasabi mayonnaise and a couple of thin slivers of raw beet.

To make the dipping sauce, mix the soy sauce and sake together and serve in a small bowl beside the sushi.

One simple ingredient can make a perfectly elegant filling for rolled sushi. Here fresh green asparagus is marinated in white miso.

miso-marinated asparagus roll

24 small or 12 medium asparagus spears

3 oz. white miso paste

2 teaspoons mirin (sweetened Japanese rice wine)

1 teaspoon wasabi paste

3 sheets of nori, halved

½ recipe seasoned sushi rice (page 9)

makes 36

Snap off any tough ends from the asparagus and discard. Bring a large saucepan of water to a boil, add the asparagus, and simmer for 3–4 minutes until tender. Drain, rinse in plenty of cold water, then let cool.

If using medium asparagus, slice each piece in half lengthwise to give 24 pieces in total. Arrange all the asparagus in a shallow dish.

Put the white miso paste, mirin, and wasabi paste in a small bowl and mix well. Spread evenly over the asparagus and let marinate for 2–4 hours.

When ready to assemble the rolls, carefully scrape the marinade off the asparagus—it should be fairly clean, so the miso doesn't overwhelm the flavor.

Put 1 half-sheet of nori, rough side up, on a rolling mat, a piece of plastic wrap, or a clean cloth. The long edge of the nori sheet should be towards you. Divide the rice into 6 portions. Spread 1 portion in a thin layer on the nori, leaving about ¾ inch bare on the far edge.

Put 4 pieces of the asparagus in a line along the middle of the rice. Lift the edge of the mat closest to you and start rolling up the sushi away from you, pressing in the filling with your fingers as you roll. You may need a little water along the far edge to seal it. Repeat to make 6 rolls in all. Using a clean, wet knife, slice each roll in half, then each half into 3, giving 6 even pieces per roll. Serve.

Rolling inside-out sushi may seem a bit hard, but it is actually very easy, because the rice on the outside molds into shape so well, and it also looks spectacular.

inside-out avocado rolls
with chives and cashews

2 small or 1 large ripe avocado

2 teaspoons lemon juice

2 tablespoons Japanese mayonnaise

¼ teaspoon salt

1 teaspoon wasabi paste (optional)

3 oz. cashews, pan-toasted (roasted salted cashews work well)

a small bunch of chives

2 sheets of nori, halved

½ recipe seasoned sushi rice (page 9)

makes 24

Peel the avocado and cut the flesh into small chunks. Put in a bowl with the lemon juice, mayonnaise, salt, and wasabi, if using. Toss and mash slightly, but not until mushy! Divide into 4 portions.

Chop the cashews very finely and put in a bowl. Chop the chives very finely and mix with the cashews. Divide into 4 portions.

Put a sheet of plastic wrap on the rolling mat. Put ½ sheet of nori on top, rough side up, with the long edge facing you. Divide the rice into 4 portions and spread 1 portion over the nori.

Sprinkle 1 portion of the nut and chive mixture on top of the rice and press it in gently with your fingers.

Carefully lift the whole thing up and flip it over so the rice is face down on the plastic wrap. Remove the sushi mat. Put 1 portion of the avocado in a line along the long edge of the nori closest to you. Carefully roll it up, then cut in half, then each half into 3, giving 6 pieces. Repeat to make 4 rolls, giving 24 pieces.

Mushrooms are a popular Japanese vegetable. Most supermarkets carry fresh shiitakes, and many may have enokis, like little clumps of white nails with tiny caps, and their bigger brothers, the hon-shigiri, with brown "berets" on their heads. If unavailable, use oyster and button mushrooms.

mushroom omelet sushi roll

4 oz. fresh shiitake mushrooms, about 12, stalks removed

4 oz. oyster mushrooms

2 oz. enoki mushrooms, roots trimmed

3 teaspoons peanut oil

1 tablespoon Japanese soy sauce

1 tablespoon mirin (sweetened Japanese rice wine)

2 eggs

¼ teaspoon salt

½ recipe seasoned sushi rice (page 9)

4 sheets of nori

a Japanese omelet pan or 10-inch skillet, preferably nonstick

makes 24–32

Slice the shiitake and oyster mushrooms into ½-inch slices. Separate the enoki mushrooms into bunches of two or three.

Heat 2 teaspoons of the oil in a large skillet and sauté the shiitake and oyster mushrooms for 2 minutes, add the enoki and stir-fry for 1½ minutes. Add the soy sauce and mirin and toss to coat. Remove from the heat and let cool. Divide into 4 portions.

Put the eggs and salt in a bowl and beat well. Heat ½ teaspoon of the oil in the pan or skillet. Slowly pour in half of the egg, tipping the pan to get an even coating. Cook for about 1 minute until set, roll up, remove from the pan, and let cool. Repeat with the remaining egg to make a second omelet. Slice the two rolled omelets in half lengthwise.

Divide the rice into 4 portions. Put 1 nori sheet on a rolling mat, rough side up, and spread with 1 portion of rice, leaving 1 inch of bare nori at the far edge. Put a strip of omelet down the middle and top with 1 portion of the mushrooms. Carefully roll up the nori in the mat, pressing the ingredients into the roll as you go. Wet the bare edge of nori and finish rolling to seal. Repeat to make 4 rolls.

Slice each roll into 6–8 pieces and serve.

Silken tofu makes a moist, tender filling—I think that firm tofu can be a bit tough. To make silken tofu a little firmer, put it in a bowl and cover it with boiling water before you start making the sushi.

broiled tofu roll

6 oz. silken tofu

2 tablespoons Japanese soy sauce

1 tablespoon mirin (sweetened Japanese rice wine)

1 teaspoon sugar

3 sheets of nori, halved (you need 5 pieces, so you will have ½ sheet left over)

1 tablespoon white sesame seeds, toasted in a dry frying pan

1 tablespoon black sesame seeds

1 tablespoon oboro (dried pink fish flakes)

½ recipe seasoned sushi rice (page 9)

1 teaspoon wasabi paste, plus extra to serve

a metal tray, lined with parchment paper

makes 24–32

Cut the tofu into ½-inch square strips and arrange in a shallow dish. Put the soy sauce, mirin, and sugar in a small bowl or small pitcher and mix well. Pour the mixture evenly over the tofu and set aside to marinate for 10 minutes.

Preheat the broiler. Put the tofu on a metal tray lined with parchment paper and broil for 2 minutes, turn the pieces over, brush with marinade. and broil for a further 2 minutes. Set aside to cool.

Cut ½ sheet of nori into tiny shreds (about 1/16-inch), put in a small bowl, and stir in the sesame seeds and oboro.

Divide the rice into 4 portions.

Spread a sheet of plastic wrap on top of the rolling mat. Put ½ sheet of nori on this and spread with 1 portion of rice. Sprinkle with one-quarter of the seed mixture, and press lightly into the rice.

Carefully lift the whole thing up and flip it over so the rice is face down on the plastic wrap. Arrange slices of broiled tofu along the long edge of the nori closest to you, smear with a little wasabi paste and carefully roll up. Repeat to make 4 rolls, then slice each roll into 6–8 pieces. Serve with extra wasabi and your choice of sushi accompaniments.

This simple little roll makes a colorful addition to a sushi plate. Try using a selection of different vegetables such as carrot, cucumber, radish, beet, and red, yellow, or orange bell peppers.

bright vegetable and thin omelet rolls

3 extra-large eggs

2 teaspoons Japanese soy sauce

2–3 teaspoons peanut oil

½ recipe seasoned sushi rice (page 9)

3 sheets of nori, halved

4 oz. mixed vegetables (see recipe introduction), very finely sliced

1 teaspoon wasabi paste (optional)

a Japanese omelet pan or 8-inch skillet

makes 36

Put the eggs and soy sauce in a bowl or small pitcher and beat well. Heat a film of oil in the omelet pan or skillet and pour in one-third of the beaten egg mixture. Swirl the egg around to cover the base of the pan and cook for about 1 minute until set. Carefully remove the omelet to a plate and cook the remaining egg mixture in 2 batches. Cut each omelet in half.

Divide the rice into 6 portions.

Put a sheet of nori on a rolling mat, rough side up, with the long edge towards you. Top with 1 portion of the rice and piece of omelet (trim the end of the omelet if it hangs over the end of the rice). Arrange a line of vegetables along the edge closest to you and smear a little wasabi, if using, in a line next to the vegetables.

Carefully roll up, brushing a little water along the edge of the nori to seal if necessary. Repeat to make 6 rolls, then slice each roll into 6 even pieces.

fish and seafood

Battleship sushi is individually hand rolled, so the nori comes about a quarter-inch above the rice, leaving room for less manageable toppings such as fish roe. Small cubes of different-colored fish make a pretty topping and you don't need to be an expert fish slicer to get tender pieces. You do, however, need very fresh raw fish—that is what "sushi- or sashimi-grade" means. If you have access to a real Japanese fishseller, that's perfect. Otherwise, go to a fish market, or other outlet where you can be sure the fish is ultra-fresh.

treasures of the sea
battleship sushi

3 oz. piece of sushi-grade raw salmon

3 oz. piece of sushi-grade raw tuna

3 oz. piece of sushi-grade raw white fish (try sea bass, turbot, or halibut)

½ recipe seasoned sushi rice (page 9)

4 sheets of nori

1 teaspoon wasabi paste (optional)

1 tablespoon salmon caviar (keta)

makes 18

Cut the salmon, tuna, and white fish into ¼-inch cubes, put them in a bowl and mix gently.

Divide the seasoned sushi rice into 18 portions, a little smaller than a table tennis ball. Gently squeeze each piece into a flattened oval shape, about 1 inch high. With dry hands, cut the nori sheets into 1-inch strips, and wrap each piece of rice in one strip with the rough side of the nori facing inwards. Seal the ends with a dab of water. You should have about ¼ inch of nori above the rice.

Put a dab of wasabi, if using, on top of the rice, then add a heaping teaspoon of the fish cubes, and a little salmon caviar.

This larger hand roll is still small enough to be held and eaten easily, but also makes a great appetizer or lunch if you allow 3 rolls per person. Choose any smoked fish, but make sure it is moist and soft.

smoked fish hand roll

1 small red onion, finely sliced

1 tablespoon rice vinegar

7 oz. smoked fish, such as trout, salmon, or eel

2-inch piece of cucumber

6 sheets of nori, about 8 x 7 inches

½ recipe seasoned sushi rice (page 9)

1 teaspoon wasabi paste (optional)

1 small carrot, finely sliced into thin strips

1 small red bell pepper, finely sliced into thin strips

makes 18

Put the onion in a small saucepan with the vinegar and ¼ cup water. Bring to a boil, drain, and let cool.

Cut the smoked fish into strips, about 2 x ½ inch—you should have about 18 even pieces.

Quarter the cucumber lengthwise, scrape out the seeds, then cut into fine strips using a mandoline or vegetable peeler.

Cut each sheet of nori into 3 pieces (3 x 7 inches).

Put a piece of nori on a work surface with the long edge towards you and the rough side up. Spread 1 small, heaping teaspoon of rice crosswise over the nori about one-quarter of the way in from the left edge. Smear with a little wasabi, if using. Top the rice with a piece of fish, a few strips of carrot, red pepper and cucumber and a little red onion, pressing slightly into the rice to hold it firm will you roll.

Take the bottom left corner of the nori and fold it diagonally so the left edge meets the top edge, continue folding the whole triangle. Arrange with the join downwards on a serving plate or tray. Repeat to make 18 rolls altogether.

Oboro are fine white fish flakes, usually colored pink, making them perfect for adding a splash of color to sushi. These tiny hand rolls are very easy to eat with your fingers, and so make perfect party food. If you mix all the ingredients before rolling the sushi, the process will be a lot easier.

california roll

3-inch piece of cucumber

6 oz. crabmeat, fresh or canned

1 small or ½ medium (firm) avocado, cut into small cubes

½ recipe seasoned sushi rice (page 9)

6–7 sheets of nori

1 teaspoon wasabi paste (optional)

1 tablespoon oboro (optional, see recipe introduction)

makes 60–70

Slice the cucumber in half lengthwise and scrape out the seeds. Chop the flesh into tiny cubes and put in a bowl. Add the crabmeat, avocado, and rice and mix gently.

Cut each sheet of nori in half lengthwise, then cut the halves into 5 pieces crosswise (4 x 1½ inches).

Put 1 piece of nori on a work surface with the long edge towards you and the rough side up. Spread 1 teaspoon of the rice mixture crosswise over the nori about one-quarter of the way in from the left edge. Smear the rice with a little wasabi, if using. Take the bottom left corner of the nori and fold it diagonally so the left edge meets the top edge, then continue folding the whole triangle. Sprinkle the open end with a little oboro, if using. Repeat until all the ingredients have been used.

The crunch of tempura batter is delicious in sushi, although the batter will soften as it cools. If you have some left-over batter, use it to cook vegetables or for the tempura croutons for miso soup on page 58.

tempura shrimp roll

24 large uncooked shrimp, peeled, but with tail fins intact

2 sheets of nori

½ recipe seasoned sushi rice (page 9)

1 teaspoon wasabi (optional)

1 cup mizuna or baby spinach

peanut or sunflower oil, for frying

tempura batter

1 egg, separated

1 tablespoon lemon juice

⅔ cup ice water

scant ⅓ cup all-purpose flour

24 bamboo skewers

makes 24

Fill a large wok or saucepan one-third full of oil and heat to 375°F, or until a small cube of bread turns golden in 30 seconds.

Thread each shrimp onto a skewer to straighten it for cooking.

To make the batter, put the egg yolk, lemon juice, and ice water in a bowl. Whisk gently, then whisk in the flour to form a smooth batter. Do not overmix.

Whisk the egg white in a second bowl until stiff but not dry, then fold into the batter.

Dip each shrimp in the batter and fry for 1–2 minutes until crisp and golden. Drain on crumpled paper towels and let cool for 5 minutes. Remove the skewers.

With dry hands, cut the nori sheets in half crosswise and then into 1-inch strips. Spread about 1 tablespoon of rice over each piece of nori, top with a tempura shrimp, a dab of wasabi, if using, and a little mizuna or baby spinach. Roll up to secure the filling. Brush the nori with water to help it stick, if necessary. Repeat until all the ingredients have been used.

Squid is delicious in sushi, but can be tricky when raw, because it does tend to be tough. If you braise it slowly, you end up with deliciously tender pieces.

slow-cooked squid

8 oz. baby squid tubes, 3 inches long (about 12), cleaned

1 teaspoon mirin (sweetened Japanese rice wine)

1 teaspoon soy sauce

½ teaspoon finely chopped fresh red chile

½ teaspoon finely chopped garlic

1 teaspoon grated fresh ginger

1 tablespoon finely chopped cilantro

½ recipe seasoned sushi rice (page 9)

1 tablespoon black sesame seeds

baking sheet with sides or broiler pan

makes 24

Slice the squid bodies in half lengthwise and arrange on a baking sheet or broiler pan. Sprinkle with the mirin and soy. Set the tray at least 6 inches away from a preheated broiler so the heat is not too fierce. Broil for about 8 minutes or until the squid turns opaque. Remove and let cool.

Put the squid in a bowl, add the chile, garlic, ginger, and cilantro, stir gently, cover, and let marinate in the refrigerator for 1 hour.

Divide the rice into 24 balls about the size of a small walnut. Top each rice ball with a piece of squid using the natural curl of the squid body to hold it securely. Sprinkle each with a few black sesame seeds, then serve.

Yakitori is the name given to food broiled on skewers over a charcoal fire. It can be anything—chicken, steak, liver, or the octopus used here. Shrimp, scallops, or any firm fish also work well. You should cook the octopus very fast over a fire to get an authentic flavor, but a hot broiler will also work.

yakitori octopus roll

6 octopus tentacles, about 2 lb, tenderized, skin and suckers removed

6 scallions

2 tablespoons sake

2 tablespoons Japanese soy sauce

1 teaspoon sugar

1 teaspoon freshly grated ginger

3 sheets of nori, halved

½ recipe seasoned sushi rice (page 9), divided into 6 portions

5 bamboo skewers, soaked in water for 30 minutes

makes 30

Cut the octopus into 1-inch pieces. Cut the scallions into 1-inch lengths. Thread the pieces of octopus and scallion crosswise alternately onto the soaked skewers.

Put the sake, soy, sugar and ginger in a small bowl or pitcher, mix well, then pour over the octopus skewers and let marinate at room temperature for 30 minutes, turning occasionally.

Preheat an outdoor grill or the broiler to very hot. Set the yakitori skewers about 3 inches from the heat and cook for 4–5 minutes, turning once. Remove from the heat and let cool.

Put a sheet of nori, rough side up, on a rolling mat, a piece of plastic wrap or a clean cloth, with the long edge towards you. Top with 1 portion of the sushi rice, spread in a thin layer, leaving about ¾ inch of bare nori on the far edge. Arrange pieces of the octopus, end to end, in a line along the middle of the rice, then put a line of scallions on top.

Lift the edge of the mat closest to you and start rolling up the sushi away from you, pressing in the filling with your fingers as you roll. You may need a little water along the far edge to seal it. Repeat to make 6 rolls. Using a clean, wet knife, slice each roll into 5 even pieces.

Note If the octopus has not been pre-tenderized, you can either beat it with a meat mallet or try this Portuguese method. Wash well and put in a large saucepan with 1 sliced onion. Cover with a lid and slowly bring to a boil over low heat (there will be enough moisture in the octopus to do this without added water). Let simmer for 30–40 minutes until the tender. Cool, then pull off and discard the purple skin and suckers.

To many sushi fans, delicious raw fish is part of the pleasure of this dish. However, if you're not an aficionado of fish *au naturel*, using smoked or pickled fish is a delicious compromise. It is very easy to pickle fish at home, and you can control the sharpness more easily.

pickled salmon roll

3 sheets of nori, halved

½ recipe seasoned sushi rice (page 9), divided into 6 portions

1 teaspoon wasabi paste (optional)

pickled salmon

½ cup rice wine vinegar

2 teaspoons salt

2 tablespoons sugar

zest of 1 unwaxed lemon, removed with a lemon zester

10 oz. salmon fillet, skinned and boned

4 shallots, finely sliced

makes 36–42

To prepare the salmon, put the vinegar, salt, sugar. and lemon zest in a saucepan with ¼ cup water. Bring to a boil, reduce the heat, then simmer for 3 minutes. Let cool.

Put the salmon fillet in a plastic container with the shallots. Pour the vinegar mixture over the top and cover tightly. Refrigerate for 2–3 days, turning the salmon in the pickle once a day.

When ready to make the sushi, drain the salmon and shallots. Slice the salmon as finely as possible and divide into 6 portions.

Put a half sheet of nori, rough side up, on a rolling mat, a piece of plastic wrap or a clean cloth, with the long edge towards you. Top with 1 portion of the sushi rice and spread it out in a thin layer, leaving about ¾ inch of bare nori at the far edge. Smear a little wasabi down the center of the rice if you like. Arrange 1 portion of the salmon slices in a line along the middle of the rice and top with a line of the pickled shallots.

Lift the edge of the mat closest to you and start rolling the sushi away from you, pressing in the filling with your fingers as you roll. You may need a little water along the far edge to seal it. Repeat with the remaining ingredients to make 6 rolls. Using a clean wet knife, slice each roll into 6–7 even pieces, then serve.

A fresh raw oyster makes such an elegantly simple topping for sushi. Chose small oysters if possible—large ones will swamp a delicate roll.

fresh oyster roll
with chile cucumber

2 sheets of nori

½ recipe seasoned sushi rice (page 9)

freshly squeezed juice of 1 lemon

20 fresh small oysters, shucked

chile cucumber

½ cup white rice vinegar

2 tablespoons sugar

1 tablespoon mirin (sweetened Japanese rice wine)

3-inch piece cucumber, halved, seeded, and cut into fine matchsticks

2 small, mild red chiles, halved, seeded, and finely sliced

makes 20

To make the chile cucumber, put the vinegar, sugar, and mirin in a small saucepan and bring to a boil, stirring. Reduce the heat and simmer for 3 minutes. Remove from the heat and let cool.

Put the cucumber and chiles in a plastic bowl and pour over the cooled vinegar mixture. Cover and refrigerate for 24 hours.

When ready to assemble the rolls, put a sheet of nori, rough side up, on a rolling mat, a piece of plastic wrap, or a clean cloth, with the long edge towards you. Add half of the sushi rice and spread it out in a thin layer, leaving about ¾ inch of bare nori on the far edge. Lift the edge of the mat closest to you and start rolling the sushi away from you. You may need a little water along the far edge to seal it. Press the roll into an oval. Repeat with the remaining ingredients to make a second roll. Using a clean, wet knife, slice each roll in half, then each half into 5 even pieces, making 20 in all.

Sprinkle lemon juice over the oysters. Top each piece of sushi with an oyster and a little chile cucumber, then serve.

Soaking in vinegar is a way of mellowing some strong-flavored fish, such as mackerel. If you don't have time to prepare fresh mackerel, try making this sushi with smoked mackerel or other smoked fish for a different, but still delicious flavor. As always, if you do use fresh mackerel, it must be very fresh indeed.

vinegared mackerel and avocado roll

1 lb. fresh mackerel fillets (about 2 medium fillets)

2 tablespoons salt

⅓ cup rice vinegar

1 tablespoon sugar

1 avocado

3 sheets of nori, halved

½ recipe seasoned sushi rice (page 9), divided into 6 portions

1 teaspoon wasabi paste (optional)

makes 36–42

Put the mackerel fillets in a shallow, non-metal bowl and sprinkle on both sides with the salt. Cover with plastic wrap and refrigerate for 8 hours or overnight.

Remove the fish from the refrigerator, rinse in cold running water, and pat dry with paper towels. Put the vinegar and sugar in a shallow dish, mix well, then add the mackerel, turning to coat. Let marinate for 40 minutes at room temperature.

Remove the fish from the marinade and slice diagonally into ½-inch strips. Slice the avocado into ½-inch strips, too.

Put a sheet of nori, rough side up, on a rolling mat, a piece of plastic wrap, or a clean cloth, with the long edge towards you. Top with 1 portion of the sushi rice and spread it out in a thin layer, leaving about ¾ inch of bare nori on the far edge. Smear a little wasabi, if using, down the middle of the rice. Arrange a line of mackerel slices over the wasabi and top with a line of the avocado.

Lift the edge of the mat closest to you and start rolling the sushi away from you, pressing in the filling with your fingers as you roll. You may need a little water along the far edge to seal it. Repeat with the remaining ingredients to make 6 rolls. Using a clean, wet knife, slice each roll into 6–7 even pieces.

Fresh tuna is one of the most popular fillings for sushi. There are three main cuts of tuna, the pink otoro (the finest), chutoro, and the dark red akami. With their incredible popularity and high price tags, otoro and chutoro are delicacies reserved for sashimi, but the akami is perfect for rolled sushi.

spicy tuna roll

10 oz. fresh tuna

2 tablespoons Japanese soy sauce

1 tablespoon sake

1 teaspoon Chinese hot pepper sauce, or chile sauce

2 scallions, finely chopped

3 sheets of nori, halved

½ recipe seasoned sushi rice (page 9), divided into 6 portions

makes 36–42 pieces

Slice the tuna into ½-inch strips and put in a shallow dish. Mix the soy sauce, sake, hot pepper sauce, and scallions in a bowl. Pour over the tuna and stir well to coat. Cover and let marinate for 30 minutes. Divide into 6 portions.

Put ½ sheet of nori, rough side up, on a rolling mat, with the long edge towards you. Top with 1 portion of the sushi rice and spread in a thin layer, leaving about ¾ inch of bare nori on the far edge. Set 1 portion of the tuna strips in a line along the middle of the rice.

Lift the edge of the mat closest to you and start rolling up the sushi away from you, pressing in the filling with your fingers as you roll. You may need a little water along the far edge to seal it. Repeat to make 6 rolls. Using a clean, wet knife, slice each roll into 6–7 even pieces.

This is a very Western idea of sushi, but I have it on good authority that it is acceptable, and also easy and convenient because it uses canned tuna. Use Japanese mayonnaise if you can, but homemade or good-quality jarred mayonnaise works well.

wasabi mayonnaise and tuna roll

4 sheets of nori

6 oz. canned albacore tuna in water, drained

4 teaspoons Japanese or other mayonnaise

1 teaspoon wasabi paste, or to taste

4 oz. baby corn, fresh or frozen, or equivalent drained canned baby corn

½ recipe seasoned sushi rice (page 9), divided into 4 portions

makes 24–28 pieces

Trim a 1-inch strip from one long edge of each sheet of nori and reserve for another use.

Put the tuna and mayonnaise in a bowl and stir in the wasabi.

If using fresh or frozen corn, bring a saucepan of water to a boil, and cook the corn for 3 minutes, or until tender. Drain and rinse under cold water to cool. If using canned corn, drain and rinse.

Set a sheet of nori, rough side up, on a rolling mat, a piece of plastic wrap, or clean cloth, with the long edge towards you. Top with 1 portion of the sushi rice, and spread it in a thin layer, leaving about ¾ inch of bare nori on the far edge. Spoon one-quarter of the tuna mixture in a line along the middle of the rice and top with a line of corn, set end to end.

Lift the edge of the mat closest to you and start rolling up the sushi away from you, pressing in the filling with your fingers as you roll. You may need a little water along the far edge to seal it. Repeat to make 4 rolls. Using a clean, wet knife, slice each roll into 6–7 even pieces.

teriyaki chicken roll
with miso dipping sauce

14 oz. boneless, skinless chicken thigh or breast (2 breasts, 4 thighs), cut into ½-inch strips

4 sheets of nori

½ recipe seasoned sushi rice (page 9) divided into 4 portions

1 teaspoon wasabi paste

teriyaki sauce

2 tablespoons Japanese soy sauce

2 tablespoons mirin (sweetened Japanese rice wine)

2 tablespoons chicken broth

teriyaki glaze

1 teaspoon sugar

½ teaspoon cornstarch

miso dipping sauce

2 tablespoons white miso paste

1 tablespoon sugar

½ cup sake

1 small egg yolk

12 bamboo skewers soaked in water for 30 minutes

makes 24–28

To make the teriyaki sauce, mix the soy, mirin and chicken broth in a small saucepan and bring to a boil. Remove from the heat and let cool.

To make the teriyaki glaze, mix the sugar and cornstarch in a small bowl with a little cold water, then stir in 2 tablespoons of the teriyaki sauce. Set aside.

Thread the strips of chicken onto the soaked skewers, then brush with half the teriyaki sauce and let marinate for about 10 minutes. Preheat a broiler or outdoor grill to very hot. Set the chicken skewers under or over the heat. Cook for 2–3 minutes, turn the skewers over, and brush with more sauce and cook for a further 2–3 minutes until cooked. Remove from the heat, pour over the teriyaki glaze, let cool, then unthread. The chicken must be cold.

Set a sheet of nori, rough side up, on a rolling mat, piece of plastic wrap, or clean cloth, with the long edge towards you. Top with one-quarter of the sushi rice, spread in a thin layer covering about half of the nori closest to you. Put one-quarter of the chicken in a line along the middle of the rice and smear with a little wasabi.

Lift the edge of the mat closest to you and start rolling up the sushi away from you, pressing in the filling with your fingers as you roll. You may need a little water along the far edge to seal it. Repeat with the remaining ingredients, to make 4 rolls. Using a clean wet knife, slice each roll into 6–7 even pieces.

To make the white miso dipping sauce, put the miso, sugar, and sake in a small saucepan over medium heat. Bring to a simmer, reduce the heat to low, and cook for 3 minutes, stirring constantly to stop it burning. Remove from the heat, quickly stir in the egg yolk, strain if necessary, and let cool before serving with the sushi.

meat and poultry

Pickled plums (umeboshi) can be bought in health food stores, Japanese and Asian supermarkets. They can be very salty and sharp, so you don't need too much. If you do not like the flavor of pickled plum, replace with pickled ginger.

sushi balls
with roast pork and pickled plums

2 tablespoons Japanese soy sauce

1 tablespoon mirin (sweetened Japanese rice wine)

1 teaspoon Chinese hot pepper sauce or chile sauce

8 oz. pork tenderloin, in one piece

½ recipe seasoned sushi rice (page 9)

10 Japanese pickled plums, halved and pitted

a roasting pan

makes 20

Put the pork in a plastic container. Mix the soy, mirin, and hot pepper sauce in a bowl or pitcher, then pour over the pork. Set aside to marinate for 1 hour, turning the pork in the marinade every 15 minutes.

Put the pork in a roasting pan and pour the marinade over the top. Roast in a preheated oven to 400°F for 15 minutes. Remove from the oven, let cool, then slice thinly—you should get about 20 slices.

Divide the rice into 20 balls. Take a piece of pickled plum and push it into the center of a rice ball, then mold the rice around it so it is completely hidden. Repeat with the remaining plums and rice. Top each ball with a slice of roast pork, then serve.

Beef tataki is very rare marinated beef served in the sashimi style. If you do not like very rare beef, cook the fillet in a preheated oven at 350°F for 10 minutes before returning to the pan to coat with sauce.

marinated beef sushi
(beef tataki)

2 teaspoons peanut oil

10 oz. beef tenderloin, in one piece

2 tablespoons Japanese soy sauce

2 tablespoons mirin (sweetened Japanese rice wine)

2 tablespoons rice vinegar

½ recipe seasoned sushi rice (page 9)

shredded pickled ginger, to serve (optional)

pickled red cabbage

about ⅛ red cabbage

½ cup brown sugar

½ cup red wine vinegar

makes 18 sushi pieces, 1 cup pickled cabbage

To make the pickled red cabbage, finely slice the cabbage, removing any large core pieces, and chop into 1-inch lengths. Put in a medium saucepan, then add the brown sugar, vinegar, and ¼ cup water. Bring to a boil, reduce the heat, and simmer for 30 minutes.

Remove from the heat, let cool, and store in a sealed container in the refrigerator for up to 1 week, or in the freezer for 3 months.

To prepare the beef, heat the oil in a skillet and sear the beef on all sides until browned. Mix the soy sauce, mirin, and vinegar in a bowl and pour over the beef, turning the beef to coat. Remove immediately from the heat and transfer the beef and its sauce to a dish. Let cool, cover, and refrigerate for 1 hour, turning once.

Divide the rice into 18 balls, the size of a walnut, and shape into firm ovals.

Cut the beef in half lengthwise (along the natural separation line), then slice as finely as possible. Wrap a piece of beef around the top of a rice ball and top with a little pickled cabbage or ginger.

miso soups

A good dashi, or soup stock, is the basis for any great miso soup. A very simple version requires only kombu and water, but fresh and dried fish give an exceptional result. Packages of little dried fish are sold in Japanese and other Asian supermarkets. Many miso pastes come premixed with dashi, but the recipes in this book call for pure miso paste—so check the package. If you do have dashi included in your paste, replace the dashi quantity with water. Different qualities of miso paste will have different strengths, so adjust quantities according to taste.

dashi and combination miso soup

1 lb. fleshy fish bones

2 tablespoons dried fish or
1 tablespoon bonito flakes

2-inch piece of kombu

combination miso soup

2 tablespoons red miso paste

2 tablespoons white miso paste

makes 6 cups dashi, soup serves 4

To make the dashi, put the fish bones, dried fish, and kombu in a large stockpot, then add 3 quarts water. Bring to a boil, reduce the heat, and simmer, partially covered with a lid, for 2 hours, skimming any foam off the top from time to time. Strain and use immediately, or cool and store in the refrigerator for up to 2 days or freeze for up to 3 months.

To make the soup, put the red miso and white miso pastes in a small bowl. Add ¼ cup dashi and stir well.

Pour 1 quart dashi in a saucepan, bring to a boil, reduce to a simmer, and stir in the miso mixture. Return to simmering point, but do not boil. Serve in 4 small bowls. (Reserve the remaining dashi for another use.)

The more mellow flavors of white miso make a perfect drink to serve with sushi rolls—the delicious and delicate taste of this soup will not overpower even the most subtle of sushi.

white miso soup
with wakame, tofu, and lettuce

a pinch of wakame (dried seaweed)

1 quart dashi stock

¼ cup white miso paste

4 oz. silken tofu, cut into ¼-inch cubes

¼ iceberg or other crisp lettuce, finely sliced (optional)

serves 4

Soak the wakame in a bowl of hot water for 15 minutes, then drain.

Pour the dashi stock in a saucepan, bring to a boil, then reduce to simmering. Mix the miso paste in a bowl with a few tablespoons of the dashi to loosen it, then stir it into the simmering stock. Add the tofu and wakame and cook in the soup for 1 minute.

Divide the lettuce, if using, between 4 bowls, ladle the hot soup over the top, then serve.

This heartier version of miso soup is perfect at the beginning or end of a sushi meal. Serve it before heavier meat- or poultry-based sushi rolls or after delicate fish or vegetarian rolls. It can also be beefed up with stir-fried vegetables as a great big bowl of soup for two.

red miso soup
with pork and noodles

8 oz. soba (buckwheat) noodles

1 quart dashi stock

1 small leek, finely sliced

3 tablespoons red miso paste

4 oz. roast pork, thinly sliced

serves 4

Fill a large saucepan three-quarters full of water and bring to a boil. Add the soba noodles and return to a boil. Add 1 cup of cold water and bring to a boil again. Boil for 3 minutes, drain, rinse in cold water, and drain again.

Pour the dashi stock in a saucepan and bring to a boil. Add the leeks and reduce to a simmer. Mix the miso paste in a bowl with a few tablespoons of the dashi to loosen it, then stir it into the simmering stock.

Divide the noodles and slices of roast pork between 4 bowls, ladle over the hot soup, then serve.

You need only about one-third of this batter for this recipe, but half an egg seems difficult to work with, so use the rest of the batter for tempura vegetables or shrimp. Alternatively, you could use the pressed croutons sold in Japanese stores.

red miso soup
with scallions and crisp tempura croutons

1 quart dashi stock

3 tablespoons red miso paste

2 scallions, finely sliced

tempura croutons

1 egg, separated

1 tablespoon lemon juice

⅔ cup ice water

⅓ cup all-purpose flour

peanut or safflower oil, for frying

serves 4

To make the batter, put the egg yolk, lemon juice, and ice water in a bowl. Whisk gently, then whisk in the flour to form a smooth batter. Do not overmix.

Whisk the egg white in a second bowl until stiff but not dry, then fold into the batter.

To cook the croutons, fill a large wok or saucepan one-third full of oil and heat to 340°F, or until a small cube of bread turns golden in 30 seconds.

Carefully drop teaspoons of the batter into the oil and cook for 30 seconds until crispy. Scoop out and drain on paper towels.

Pour the dashi into a saucepan, bring to a boil, then reduce to a simmer. Mix the miso paste with a few tablespoons of the dashi to loosen it, then stir it into the simmering stock. Divide the stock between 4 bowls, add the croutons and scallions, and serve.

pickled ginger

6 oz. piece of fresh ginger

1 tablespoon salt

½ cup rice vinegar

½ cup plus 1 tablespoons sugar

1 slice fresh beet, 1 red radish, sliced, or a drop of red food coloring (optional)

makes about 1 cup

Peel the ginger and slice it very finely with a mandoline or vegetable peeler. Put it in a large strainer or colander and sprinkle with salt. Set aside for 30 minutes, then rinse thoroughly.

Put the rice vinegar and sugar in a saucepan, add ¼ cup water, and bring to a boil, stirring until the sugar has dissolved. Boil for 5 minutes. Let cool, then pour over the ginger. If you would like it to be pink, like store-bought ginger, add the beet, radish, or food coloring.

Cover and refrigerate for at least 24 hours or until needed.

Pickled ginger is the traditional companion for sushi. The subtle flavoring of raw fish, delicate rice, and fresh vegetables can easily be overpowered by the lingering flavors of previous morsels. Ginger helps cleanse the palate, introducing a sharp freshness that stimulates the taste buds for the next delight.

accompaniments

mixed pickles

Other vegetables can be pickled and served with sushi alongside ginger. They look wonderfully colorful, adding a touch of drama to your sushi platter, making it appear very professional.

½ cucumber, about 4 inches long

1 carrot, about 3 oz.

3 oz. daikon radish, peeled, or 6 red radishes

¼ small green cabbage, about 6 oz.

6 garlic cloves, thinly sliced

1 tablespoon salt

½ lemon, sliced

1 cup rice vinegar

1 cup sugar

makes about 2 cups

Cut the cucumber in half lengthwise and scoop out the seeds. Slice the cucumber, carrot, and radish into very thin strips.

Slice the cabbage into ½-inch strips. Put all the vegetables and garlic in a colander, sprinkle with salt, and toss well. Set aside for 30 minutes, then rinse thoroughly and top with the sliced lemon.

Put the rice vinegar and sugar in a saucepan with ½ cup water. Bring to a boil, stirring until the sugar has dissolved. Boil for 5 minutes. Let cool, then pour over the vegetables and lemon. Cover and chill for at least 24 hours or until needed. Keeps for 1 month in the refrigerator.

wasabi paste

Most of the wasabi we buy in tubes is a mixture of horseradish and wasabi—or it can be just horseradish dyed green. If you buy wasabi paste from a Japanese market, you will have a selection of various qualities, and it is always best to buy the best.

Many Japanese cooks prefer to mix their own paste from silver-grey wasabi powder, sold in small cans, like paprika, believing that the flavor is stronger and sharper. The fresh roots are not widely available, even in Japan, but if you see them in a speciality greengrocer, sold on a bed of ice, do try them. To experience the real flavor and rush of wasabi you can make your own paste from them. It is traditionally grated using a sharkskin grater, but a porcelain ginger grater or a Microplane® will also work. After grating, the heat in wasabi lasts for only about 10 minutes, so you must use it right away.

wasabi from powder

1 teaspoon wasabi powder

serves 1

Put the wasabi powder in a small bowl, such as an eggcup. Add 1 teaspoon water and mix with the end of a chopstick. Serve immediately.

fresh wasabi paste

1 fresh wasabi root

a wasabi grater or other fine grater

serves 6–8

Scrape or peel off the rough skin from the root. Using a circular motion, rub the wasabi gently against an abrasive grater onto a chopping board. Pound and chop the grated wasabi to a fine paste with a large knife or cleaver. Consume within 10 minutes.

Note To keep the wasabi from discoloring for as long as possible, turn the little bowl upside down until serving—this will stop the air getting at it.

index

conversion charts

Weights and measures have been rounded up or down slightly to make measuring easier.

Volume equivalents:

American	Metric	Imperial
1 teaspoon	5 ml	
1 tablespoon	15 ml	
¼ cup	60 ml	2 fl.oz.
⅓ cup	75 ml	2½ fl.oz.
½ cup	125 ml	4 fl.oz.
⅔ cup	150 ml	5 fl.oz. (¼ pint)
¾ cup	175 ml	6 fl.oz.
1 cup	250 ml	8 fl.oz.

Weight equivalents: Measurements:

Imperial	Metric	Inches	Cm
1 oz.	25 g	¼ inch	5 mm
2 oz.	50 g	½ inch	1 cm
3 oz.	75 g	¾ inch	1.5 cm
4 oz.	125 g	1 inch	2.5 cm
5 oz.	150 g	2 inches	5 cm
6 oz.	175 g	3 inches	7 cm
7 oz.	200 g	4 inches	10 cm
8 oz. (½ lb.)	250 g	5 inches	12 cm
9 oz.	275 g	6 inches	15 cm
10 oz.	300 g	7 inches	18 cm
11 oz.	325 g	8 inches	20 cm
12 oz.	375 g	9 inches	23 cm
13 oz.	400 g	10 inches	25 cm
14 oz.	425 g	11 inches	28 cm
15 oz.	475 g	12 inches	30 cm
16 oz. (1 lb.)	500 g		
2 lb.	1 kg		

Oven temperatures:

110°C	(225°F)	Gas ¼
120°C	(250°F)	Gas ½
140°C	(275°F)	Gas 1
150°C	(300°F)	Gas 2
160°C	(325°F)	Gas 3
180°C	(350°F)	Gas 4
190°C	(375°F)	Gas 5
200°C	(400°F)	Gas 6
220°C	(425°F)	Gas 7
230°C	(450°F)	Gas 8
240°C	(475°F)	Gas 9